Launched in

Eternity

Twenty true stories of crime and punishment in Derby and Derbyshire

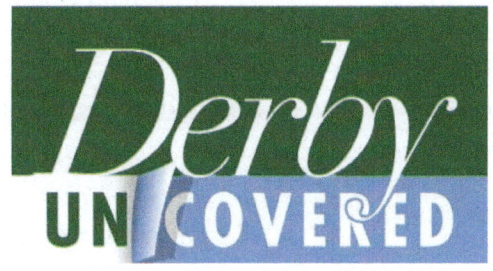

First published in 2022

Derby Uncovered Group
76 Bramfield Avenue
Derby, Derbyshire, DE22 3TL
www.derbyuncovered.com

CONTENTS

Introduction.

Being a proud citizen of Derby all my life, it has perhaps been easy to fall into the trap of being biased about my home city and county. When I first started to investigate the history of Derbyshire in my early twenties, it seemed that Derby and Derbyshire had an unusual amount of both fascinating stories and characters woven into its fabric. At first, part of me dismissed this as natural bias, but the more I looked, the more I realised that I was correct all along.

Numerous people who went on to change the world in ways we still see today were either from Derby or Derbyshire or had strong connections in their personal or business lives here.

It also struck me that Derbyshire seemed to have an abundance of true crime stories and, in particular, some really fascinating stories behind those crimes.

This is my attempt to bring you some of my particular favourite tales of the crimes of long ago and their often unbelievably cruel punishments.

I have lots of people, (and one pet), to thank for this book – my fiancée and business partner Jeni, my children Annabelle and Jamie, and my faithful dog Dante, all of whom, at some points, have had to put up with my inherent grumpiness while I worked on this project. My thanks also go to all of my friends that have supported me during not just the writing of this book but also the launch of Derby Uncovered.

Great thanks, of course, also go to all the authors, historians and researchers on this subject who went before me – any mistakes are mine and mine alone.

David Turner
DERBY UNCOVERED

The Bakewell Witches.

"Days had been when all men – save Macbeth – feared witches."

Modern Day Bakewell.

Credit: Roger Cornfoot / Floral roundabout, Bakewell

Nowadays we perhaps take our scientific knowledge for granted but this was not always the case. While we may have a passing awareness of the superstitious beliefs of hundreds of years ago, we may not be aware of the very real consequences those beliefs had for some people.

For example, when it came to those unfortunate women accused of witchcraft, those beliefs often had deadly consequences for those found guilty.

In 1590-91, four witches of North Berwick were burnt at the stake in Edinburgh after being convicted of conspiring to murder King James VI, (later to become James I of Great Britain), and his queen Anne of Denmark. It is doubtful, of course, that any trial these four unfortunate women received would have been fair, but James himself was a firm believer in witchcraft. He even wrote a tract on *'Demonologie'* which he claimed provided evidence to demonstrate the reality of witches.

Consequently, when he became King of England in 1603, he persuaded Parliament to pass an Act against *"Conjuration, Witchcraft and Dealing with Evil and Wicked Spirits."*

A short time later, c.1607, a certain Mrs. Stafford and another female, possibly either her friend or sister with whom she lived, would tragically fall victim to the hysteria and superstitions that were widespread at the time. These superstitions were so widespread in fact, that it is estimated that in England alone, between 500 and 1,000 people were executed after being accused of witchcraft and 90 percent of those were women.

Mrs. Stafford, a milliner, lived with a female companion in Bakewell. To supplement her income, she would take in lodgers from time to time. On one occasion a travelling Scotsman had taken his lodgings in her home. Falling behind on his rent he was evicted and Mrs. Stafford kept his belongings in lieu of his debt. This was to prove very costly to both her and her companion.

The former lodger turned up next, when a watchman discovered him dressed in rags and hiding in a London cellar. He was arrested for being in an unoccupied house with felonious intent and brought before the magistrates in London.

The accused man told the magistrate that he had arrived in London *'by magic'*. Claiming his innocence, he explained that he had been awoken in his room in Bakewell by a bright light shining through the gaps in the floorboards. Peeking through the gaps, he claimed to have seen Mrs. Stafford and her companion dressed in outdoor clothes and chanting a spell:

"Over thick, over thin,

"Now Devil, to the cellar in Lunnon."

According to his incredulous claims, he found himself repeating the lines, at which point he was immediately caught up in a hurricane and whirled away until he found himself in his ragged nightshirt by the side of the witches in a cellar lit by a dim lamp. The *'witches'*, he claimed, were busy tying up parcels of silks and other goods which he assumed they had *'lifted'* from shops that they had passed on their hurricane-fuelled flight to London.

He further claimed that he had fallen unconscious after drinking wine which had been given to him by Mrs. Stafford. His excuse for his ragged attire was that his clothes were still in Mrs. Stafford's house in Bakewell – which, as she had kept his belongings, was undoubtedly true.

It is obvious looking back, that the accused man was up to no good and that the two women were simply, and callously, the scapegoats of the man. However, in those times such fanciful

7

accusations were taken very seriously, and the magistrate, agreeing that this was a case of witchcraft, ordered that the justices of Derbyshire were to be provided with the information.

The falsely accused women were apprehended, tried and executed.

It seems barely credible nowadays that such a claim would be believed but these were very different times indeed. These were the times where a young man would choose to be the executioner of both his older brother and father to spare his own life.

John Crossland – the man who hung his own family.

"So void of feeling for distress, he rejoiced at a murder, because it brought the prospect of a guinea."

When we look back on the history of crime and punishment in Derby, one of the people who often gets only a small mention, but is there every time, is the executioner or the hangman. As we go back further and further in time it's hard to find barely any information on the people responsible for ending the lives of so many others.

In fact, only one early Derbyshire hangman has ever been identified with any degree of certainty. His name was John Crossland and through his actions he would enter infamy.

You might, and who would blame you, make the mistake of thinking that John himself was an upstanding citizen. After all, he was responsible for sending so many people convicted of their crimes to meet their maker. If you thought this though, then I am afraid that you would be very wrong indeed.

During the time of Oliver Cromwell's reign, (1653 to 1658), John himself was tried at the Derby Assizes for horse stealing. Standing alongside him, and accused of the same crime, were his father and older brother. Perhaps we can read from this that John's family were, in fact, seasoned criminals, or maybe, just as so many crimes in those times were, their crime had been borne out of poverty.

None of this made any difference to the bench who found them guilty and sentenced them to death by hanging. In a more enlightened age we might, of course, find that shocking but what happened after the sentence was passed is on another level altogether.

As the historian and poet William Hutton, (1723 – 1815), said in his *'History of Derby'* which was published in 1791: *"When Power wantons in cruelty, it becomes detestable, and gives greater offence than even the culprits."*

The cruelty in question was the offer from the bench, that due to lacking an official hangman at that time, if one of the three should hang the other two, then they would themselves be pardoned.

The offer was placed first to the father who, of course, declined:

"Was it ever known that a father hanged his children?" he asked, *"How can I take away those lives which I have given, have cherished, and which, of all things, are the most dear?"*

The offer was then made to the eldest son and was again declined:

"Though life is the most dear of all possessions, yet even that may be purchased too dear," he said.

Turning to John, the bench made the offer to him last. John accepted the offer with an *'avidity'* that led William Hutton to observe: *"He would hang half the creation, and even the judges, rather than be a sufferer himself."*

William Hutton, (1723-1815) chronicled many of the details regarding John Crossland in his 1791 book – 'History of Derby'.

Looking back through the microscope of time it's hard to comprehend that the judges would have even contemplated making such an offer, but the offer was made, and John accepted it.

With no remorse whatsoever, he performed the executions, and performed them so well, that he was awarded the job of hangman for Derby and two or three neighbouring counties.

Hutton described John as, *'loving none, and beloved by none'*, and it is reported that when seen in the streets he would be pelted with objects easy to hand. His callousness was so well known that Hutton reported that parents would threaten any disobedient children by merely using his name.

John died around 1705 and we neither know who proceeded him, nor do we know who succeeded him. Perhaps as the story of the only confirmed hangman for Derbyshire shows us – it's best that we don't.

It was certainly a different world then. A world where a man called Noah in Derby built his very own ark.

Noah Bullock and Derby's very own ark.

"He built an ark, and launched it upon the Derwent."

The Noah's Ark public house in Derby.

Pretty much all of us, whether religious or not, and whatever religion we are, know the story of Noah and his ark. What most people don't know is that Derby had its very own Noah – and he built his very own ark.

His name was Noah Bullock and our Noah's motivations for building an ark were somewhat different.

In the 1600s in Derby, as it was everywhere in the UK, counterfeiting was a lucrative, yet dangerous business. Get caught and you might face the hangman's noose.

Noah was a counterfeiter but not just an average one, he was also a 'clipper'. Clipping involved taking a small amount of metal off the edge of hand-struck coins. Over time, the precious metal clippings could be saved up and melted into bullion to be sold or used to make new coins.

As you might imagine, what every counterfeiter and clipper needed was a safe and secure place to commit their crimes and Noah, perhaps guided by his name, had just the plan.

Building an ark, he moored it on the River Derwent, near to where the Morledge is now. Whether he lived in the ark with his family is not known, and he certainly wouldn't have had to face the huge waves and life at sea the original Noah faced, but it was certainly the base of his illicit operations.

As with many criminals, Noah's crimes eventually caught up with him and the ark that he'd built didn't offer the same level of protection as the one built by the biblical Noah. It was only a case of the familiar adage – it's not what you know, but who you know – that would ultimately save him.

In 1676, Noah was caught and hauled up before the authorities. Many before him and many after him were sent to meet their maker for the types of crimes he had undoubtedly committed, however the recorder of Derby was a certain Sir Simon Degge.

Sir Simon wasn't a stranger to controversy and problems with the law himself. He had been arrested as a Royalist during the Long Parliament, and after he was knighted, was twice fined by the courts for failing to do his duties. Sir Simon and Noah knew each other, and to escape the hangman Noah promised to stop his illegal activities and to destroy his ark. The ark was duly broken up and sank in the River Derwent.

Established in the first half of the 1700s, the Noah's Ark Public House in The Morledge is believed to be named after Derby's very own Noah. It is said that the ghostly figure of Noah Bullock has been spotted there and in the surrounding area.

As those of you who know Derby, it's just a short walk from the Morledge to the Market Place. That, for a long time, was the location of the Pillory in Derby. This was a small timber platform which was elevated away from the floor so as to place the victim in full view of the public, who could throw rotten vegetables (and often much worse) at the victim.

It was also the place where, only a few decades after the natural death of Noah Bullock in 1687, the notorious and despised Ellen Beare was placed in the pillory for endeavouring to persuade a man to murder his wife, for procuring an abortion with the use of a skewer and for destroying the foetus of an unnamed woman. She was also locally despised for her involvement in another murder that left a young woman dead and two others executed.

The notorious Ellen Beare.

"New kennels provided new ammunition; and she became a moving heap of filth."

Ellen Beare was described by the historian William Hutton as 'handsome', and she certainly was well sought after. Whether this was due to her looks, her personality or the services she could help with, it is very much open to debate.

Landlady of the Crown Inn on Nuns' Green, she could perform abortions and could also provide the means to help a man dispose of his wife – usually with poison.

Although married to a man called Ebenezer, he carried no weight or say in either their relationship or their establishment and, according to Hutton, he had 'no more influence over her than a mouse over a cat.'

It was at the Crown Inn that Rosamond Olleranshaw worked as a serving maid. It was also at the Crown Inn that John Hewitt, a butcher, aged around 30, from Stepping Lane, and his wife Hannah drank, and it was in the Crown Inn that the seeds of Hannah's ultimate demise would be sown in 1732.

The marriage of John and Hannah was not a happy one. John was violent and kept his wife short of money and even the birth of a daughter had done nothing to improve their union of seven years. Although they drank at the Crown Inn they did so separately and it was here that Rosamond formed an attachment with John, perhaps naively believing his tall tales of how his relationship issues were all the fault of his wife. Between the three of them – Beare, Hewitt and Olleranshaw – a plot was hatched to help John dispose of his wife.

Probably due to the John Hewitt-imposed shortage of money, Hannah was said to have always looked undernourished. So, when Ellen Beare offered her a meal of pancakes it was more than understandable that she eagerly agreed. The pancakes were made by Ellen and served to Hannah by Rosamond. Within just three hours of eating them, Hannah was dead.

As Hutton described it 'the neighbours cried Foul play!' and after Hannah's body was examined by a coroner, enough arsenic to kill half-a-dozen people was found inside her. All three of the conspirators were arrested and at the assizes Hewitt, showing a previously very well-hidden streak of chivalry, attempted to help Rosamond.

According to Hutton:

"For the judge having asked her (Rosamond) whether Mrs. Beare was privy to the poisoning or ordered her to administer it, John trod upon her toe in order that she might tell the truth and save herself, but she unfortunately mistook the hint for its reverse and answered 'No'; by which she saved the life of her mistress and lost her own."

John Hewitt and Rosamond Olleranshaw were executed on March 29, 1732.

As soon as the executions were over all attention turned to Ellen. Three days after the executions the Mayor of Derby ordered the digging up of her garden at the Crown Inn. Whomsoever gave him the tip is unknown, but the bones of a child aged around seven to eight months were discovered. At the July assizes of the same year, she stood to face more charges, although strangely none of the charges related to the bones found in her garden. Instead, she was charged with:

1.   Endeavouring to help a man named Nicholas Wilson murder his wife.

2.   Procuring an abortion for a woman named Grace Belfort, where she charged a fee of five guineas and used an iron skewer.

3.   Destroying the foetus of an unnamed woman.

Although the third charge was ultimately not proceeded with, she was found guilty of the first two and sentenced to stand in the pillory for an hour at the next two market days in Derby and to serve three years in prison.

On August 18 she was forcibly dragged to the pillory for her first hour. William Hutton himself, young but part of the witnessing crowd, wrote: *"All the apples, eggs, and turnips that caught be bought, begged, or stolen, were directed at her devoted head. The stagnate kennels were robbed of their contents, and became the cleanest part of the street."*

With the pillory at the time needing repairs, Ellen managed to release herself and ran down the Morledge, being pelted every step of the way where *'new kennels provided new ammunition; and she became a moving heap of filth.'* Upon her recapture she was placed back in the pillory for the remainder of her session and at the end of it was taken back to prison.

The Ellen Beare that returned for her second visit to the pillory was a very different woman. No longer the proud and confident young woman of previous times, she had the appearance of being old and decrepit. Her deviousness was still apparent though when she was found to be wearing numerous extra layers of clothing and a pewter plate to protect her head. With this removed she endured her second visit to the pillory before being taken back to prison to serve her three-year sentence.

An example of the pillory.
Credit: Green, Tim. Pillory at Barley Hall, York. December 16, 2007. Photograph. Flickr.
https://www.flickr.com/photos/atoach/2115696140/

And what became of Ellen? Did the three years she served dampen her criminal nature?

By all accounts she recovered her health and looks but her nature stayed the same. After being released in August 1735, with the fickle-minded public greeting her outside the prison with a welcoming party complete with a band, she was soon remanded back in prison on a charge of receiving stolen goods – a charge for which she would serve one year. Hutton though, recalls that despite her numerous brushes with the law she ultimately died in *'the meridian of life'*.

The tragic victim, Hannah, wasn't the only murder victim to die of poisoning in Derby. Others did too, and if the stories told are to be believed, then one of those victims played a part in one of the very first cases of industrial espionage in the world.

John Lombe – an early industrial spy.

"who lingered two or three years in agonies, and departed."

The Museum of Making in Derby.
Credit: Matt Brown, CC BY 2.0, via Wikimedia Commons

When we consider industrial espionage and spying nowadays, it's tempting for our minds to think of high-tech things. After all, we regularly read articles in the news warning us of the danger of cyber-attacks from places such as Russia, China and North Korea. We are also warned about the modern-day phenomenon of ransomware. This is where fraudsters install rogue software on companies' computer systems that may well stop them accessing vital files which are necessary for them to do business. The rogue files are only removed once the ransom has been paid – and this has become a worryingly frequent occurrence. However, although the technology used to perform these crimes is very much a modern-day thing, the urge and desire to cheat in the business world is not.

This story starts in Norwich, England, in 1693. It was here that John Lombe was born, the son of a weaver. In the early 18th century the demand for spun silk was outstripping supply within the textile industry, and John had obtained employment at an ultimately unsuccessful mill in Derby owned by Thomas Cotchett. Whilst this was happening, over in Piedmont, in north-west Italy, the Italians had developed their own secret technologies and practices in this field. This exclusive knowledge in the art of silk throwing gave them a monopoly on this growing and lucrative market. As the historian William Hutton said: *"The wear of silks was the taste of the ladies; and the British merchant was obliged to apply to the Italian, with ready money, for the article at an exorbitant price."*

In 1716, Thomas Lombe sent his half-brother John over to Italy to investigate. Upon his arrival, John managed to bribe a priest to find him work in a local silk manufactory, where he worked during the day as a machinery mechanic. Knowing that the Italians kept their methods incredibly secret, in the words of William Hutton, John had *'adopted the usual mode of accomplishing his end by corrupting the servants'* and, alongside the servants, returned at night in private where he took copious notes and sketches by candlelight.

Hutton goes on to further say that when the plot was discovered, John *'fled, with the utmost precipitation, on board a ship, at the hazard of his life, taking with him two natives, who had favoured his interest and his life at the risk of their own.'*

With the necessary knowledge and with the aid of the Italians who had returned with him, John and his half-brother Thomas designed a mill and commissioned George Sorocold to build it and install the new machines. George built the mill between 1717 and 1721 and in 1718, Thomas managed to obtain a 14-year British patent *for 'A New Invention of Three Sorts of Engines never before made or used in Great Britaine, One to Wind the Finest Raw Silk, Another to Spin, and the Other to Twist the Finest Italian Raw Slik into Organzine in great Perfection, which was never before done in this Kingdom'.*

The factory became the first successful powered continuous production unit in the world and was the model for the factory concept used by Sir Richard Arkwright and others in the Industrial Revolution, attracting visitors such as Daniel Defoe and Benjamin Franklin.

Many years later, in 1891, the main building was almost destroyed in a fire. Another fire badly damaged the building in 1910 – at this point it was rebuilt in the form we see today where it now houses Derby's excellent Museum of Making.

But what of John? How did he spend the fortune he so surely amassed from such a successful venture?

The answer is he didn't get to do so. Seeking revenge, the Italians sent over a female assassin who successfully integrated herself with one of the workers. *"By these two,"* says Hutton, *"slow poison was supposed, and perhaps justly, to have been administered to John Lombe, who lingered two or three years in agonies, and departed."*

The assassin was never found and evaded the law. Many years later a man named Gerald Mainwaring – tried to evade justice by shooting PC Joseph Moss, the only Derby police constable to ever be killed on active duty in Derby. By doing so, he not only ended the life of PC Moss, but also inadvertently caused a scandal when his own life was decided based on a lottery.

Gerald Mainwaring – a lottery of life and death.

"Stop, I'll have no more of this."

A postcard image of the Royal Hotel in Derby c.1905.

On July 12, 1879, as PC Joseph Moss went about his day neither he, nor indeed anybody else, could have expected the dramatic and tragic events that were about to unfold. For, before the end of the day, he would become the first, and at this point in time, only Derby police constable to ever be killed on active duty in Derby.

Unbeknownst to him, a certain Gerald Mainwaring was staying nearby at The Royal Hotel in Derby. Described at the time by the Derby Mercury as, '*a person of birth and education*', he was the seventh of ten children of the late Reverend Charles Henry Mainwaring of Whitmore Hall, Staffordshire, a respected magistrate whose wife Jane Broughton descended from Broughton Hall, Staffordshire. We can deduct from many of the reports of him that Mainwaring saw himself as somewhat above the law – indeed while he was staying at The Royal Hotel, Mainwaring had purchased 300 rounds of ammunition for a revolver that his brother had given him.

It was on July 12 that he got drunk with a woman called Annie Green. Some reports from the time have described her as a prostitute although this was never confirmed. What was known is that she lived on the now no-longer Bradshaw Street – now Bradshaw Way in Derby. It was here that Gerald and Annie spent a lot of their time.

On that fateful Saturday, Gerald had brought to him a horse and trap that he had previously hired at the White Hart in Ashbourne. Seen doing something that looked very much like him loading his gun, he took the trap to Bradshaw Street where he proceeded to encourage a drunken Annie to get in with him. The woman who kept the house – Sophia Gilbert - attempted to stop Annie, only to be threatened by the armed Gerald.

Making their way into the town centre, Gerald's erratic driving was spotted by PC John Stamp and as Gerald drove around the corner of the Cornmarket and Victoria Street, the PC attempted to stop him. Gerald refused to stop so PC Stamp, alongside PC John Shirley and PC Joseph Moss, pursued him and Annie on foot as the trap headed towards Ashbourne Road.

The pursuit was finally concluded at the Traveller's Rest at the top of the road and Mainwaring was arrested. It was at this point that Annie became violent and they were both taken to Derby Borough Police Lock-Up in the Cornmarket.

Whilst Annie resisted the policemen, Gerald, who up to this point had been relatively subdued and crucially was not handcuffed, pulled the revolver out of his pocket and shouted: *"Stop, I'll have no more of this!"* and fired four shots in a room only around 8 feet by 10 feet in size. One of the shots hit PC Joseph Moss in the side, one knocked PC Price's helmet off and another hit him in the arm. When Mainwaring was eventually overpowered the injured officers were taken to the Derby Infirmary.

At 12.55pm on July 13, PC Joseph Moss, (a former Grenadier Guard), died from his injuries and was buried with full military honours.

Mainwaring was tried at the Derby Assizes for wilful murder and found guilty – Mr Justice Lindsay pronounced the death sentence and the matter was referred to the Home Secretary for a final decision. There was no strong expectation for any form of reprieve. It was at this point that some deeply disturbing news emerged.

It was disclosed by some jury members that the jury had been spilt into two groups of six, one of which wanted a verdict of manslaughter and the other wanted a verdict of wilful murder. In addition to this, the jury chairman had refused to deliver a decision, so the choice was made to draw lots to elect a new chairman who would enact a casting vote – in this case murder.

The story reached the national press, who true to form embellished it, proclaiming that the guilty verdict had *'been decided on the toss of a coin'*. The case was even debated in Parliament. The effect of this seemed to obscure to some of the public the very nature of the original crime and a petition was launched in Derby demanding the death sentence be remitted as Gerald had been wronged by the jury – 5,720 people signed it.

In the end Gerald did have his sentence of death commuted and he served 15 years in prison before being released. His precise movements after that are unknown though many believe he went to either America or Canada. The case became known as 'The Great Jury Scandal' and led to many people looking into what changes might be needed to improve the jury system.

That the shooting of PC Joseph Moss was a despicable crime is not, and never has been, a source of debate, but the repercussions of his trial were felt nationwide.

Over the previous centuries there were indeed many flaws with the legal system but that wasn't all that the accused needed to be concerned about. If you were standing with one or more co-accused, there was a chance that one of them might turn King's evidence - giving information (such as the names of other criminals) to the court in order to reduce one's own punishment when one has been charged with a crime. In 1679 it was not one, but two people, who turned King's evidence, resulting in Derbyshire's largest mass hanging.

The Bracy Gang – stand and deliver.

"It hath not been unknown to most persons Travelling the great Roads of England, how they have been infested of late with Highway-Men or Robbers."

An illustration of a highwaymen of olden times.
Credit: Edgar Alfred Holloway, Public domain, via Wikimedia Commons.

When many people think of highwaymen, perhaps the first one to spring to mind is the often dramatised and romanticised Richard 'Dick' Turpin. As with many things though, this approach can deter the viewer from knowing and understanding the often very violent nature of these individuals. Most highwaymen had no element of romance to them and were callous individuals who would torture and kill if necessary.

One of the most notorious gangs of highwaymen to plague Derby and Derbyshire, as well as Nottingham and Newark, was the Bracy Gang.

The leader of the gang was a Nottinghamshire man named Richard Bracy. With a varied criminal record by the age of 18, and suspected of the murder of a servant girl when he was 17, Richard was an unsavoury character who was unmoved at the prospect of torturing his victims if they did not cooperate.

The members of his 'gang' - Richard Piggen, Roger Brookham, Joseph Gerrat, John Barker, William Loe, John Roobottom, Thomas Ouldome, John Baker, Daniel Buck, Thomas Gillat, and Andrew Smedley - have left only their recorded names and their crimes to the ledgers of history.

Before their ultimate demise, the Bracy Gang members could consider themselves to have been very successful. They seem to have begun their joint activities around 1677, including a robbery at the house of *"Captain John Munday Esquire, near the Town of Derby, at a place called Morton; where they took away to the value of 1200 pounds in Gold and Silver, besides a great quantity of Plate, binding the Esquire and all his Family in their Beds, and using great insolencies by threats, to make them confess their Treasures, which they obtained and secured at the present."*

Note that £1,200 in today's money would be worth around £180,000.

Covering Derbyshire and Nottinghamshire, their targets ranged far and wide, including just outside of Derby in Ockbrook. Unafraid to kill to protect the interests of their gang, they killed a young boy aged around fifteen who overheard them planning a raid in a local inn and, *'hid him in a Vault, and afterwards made their escape with one Widdow Rose of Lenton, near Nottingham, who entertained them.'*

Their demise began when Richard Bracy was ambushed at his wife's inn after one of the servants there tipped off a Justice of the Peace. With their leader gone, the remaining 11 members of his gang attempted to carry on with their brutal and illegal activities but, one by one, they were caught until they were all arraigned to appear at the Derby Assizes in August 1679.

As with many bonds forged through crime during the era of the death sentence, the will to survive proved to be stronger than the bond of any type of relationship, and both John Piggen and John Baker turned King's evidence and testified against the others.

Richard Bracy and the remaining nine members of the gang were hanged in what would have been the biggest multiple hanging in the county's history. One man would have been particularly happy about his payday for this – John Crossland – Derby's notorious and despised hangman.

It seems that the countless executions performed in the past were not enough to deter some people from a life of crime and every so often other deterrents were put in place. On occasions one of these was the gibbeting of the body involving a gallows-type contraption on which the victim's executed body would be put on public display to deter other existing or potential criminals. This was the fate of a man named Anthony Lingard in 1815.

Anthony Lingard – the last gibbeting in Derbyshire.

"and the necessity of presenting an awful example to them."

The Three Stags Head in Wardlow, opposite the site of the tollhouse and the scene of the

murder of Hannah Oliver.

Credit: Jon, CC BY 2.0, via Wikimedia Commons.

Born in Tideswell, Anthony Lingard was one of several children born to his father Anthony Lingard Snr and his mother, Elizabeth. By his early twenties he had developed a reputation, in and around where he lived in Litton, Derbyshire, of being a man of low morals and even lower sexual restraint. It should, therefore, come as no surprise to learn that, despite him having no means to provide for a child, he still managed to get a local woman – Rebecca Nall – pregnant.

Finding himself in this predicament, Anthony took it upon himself to go and visit a woman called Hannah Oliver – the tollhouse keeper at Wardlow Mires. What his initial motives were are unclear, but his visit resulted in a vicious argument that ended Hannah's life.

According to the evidence given at the time, on the night of January 15, 1815, Anthony entered Hannah's house and after killing her he left with her money and a new pair of shoes. He then offered the money and shoes to the pregnant Rebecca and, in return, she would say that someone else was the father of her baby.

Once Hannah's body was discovered by a maidservant from The Three Stags Head – an inn across the road from the tollhouse – news spread fast. Upon hearing the news Rebecca immediately returned the shoes to Anthony. After first trying to hide them in a haystack near his residence in Litton, he later retrieved them which proved to be a very costly mistake as he was eventually caught in possession of the shoes.

With the evidence overwhelmingly insurmountable, Anthony made a full confession and was sentenced to death. The Derby Mercury at the time described Anthony as *'but one remove from the brute creation, being absolutely devoid of religious knowledge, having no concern whatsoever about the future, and not to be reached by any of the ministrations of the chaplain.'*

It was common at the time, that after the body had been executed it would be dissected, but this did not happen in this case. The court ruled that Anthony's corpse would instead be gibbeted – hung in chains – as a warning to others. The sentence was duly carried out on March 28, 1815 and Anthony's body was taken to a location somewhere between Peter's Stone – a limestone outcrop in Wardlow Mires – and the main road nearby.

Anthony's remains were to hang there, acting as a warning to other would-be criminals, for 11 years until a local magistrate ordered that the gibbet be dismantled.

Through either fate, irony, or a combination of the two, his remains were hanging there long enough to witness his brother, William Lingard, attack and rob travellers on the nearby road alongside a man named William Bennett. His brother also received the death penalty, but luckily for William, he was reprieved.

More than ironically, and perhaps fantastically coincidentally, the rotting remains also witnessed one more thing – the sight of Hannah Bocking, herself only a child of 16, poisoning her young female companion, Jane Grant by means of a sweet cake laced with arsenic.

Hannah Bocking – the 16-year-old murderess.

"a mind greatly darkened and depraved."

Based on their locations, the murders committed by Hannah Bocking and Anthony Lingard – who we covered in our last instalment – must have occurred in extremely close proximity.

The victim of Hannah's crime was a female of a similar age to her – Jane Grant. Even throughout the passage of time we have always, and understandably, regarded child killers with a level of bewilderment and shock.

How could someone so young commit such a crime?

We look at what they did and hope that we can find something in them that can perhaps help us sleep better. In the case of the murder of Jane Grant we unfortunately can't find anything to help us with the night hours. This murder was premeditated, carefully planned and callously executed.

Both Hannah and Jane had applied for a household servant's position. When Hannah was rejected due to her *'unamiable temper and disposition'*, and Jane had been accepted to the position, it was the only catalyst required to trigger her evil plan. With a level of deviousness that belied her young years, she first spent time befriending Jane and gaining her trust. When she felt this had been achieved, she procured arsenic from the neighbourhood surgeon, telling him that it was for her grandfather to kill rats. She even had the foresight to take along with her a young man in case the surgeon would not sell it to her alone.

Mixing the poison into a cake, and with the girls now firm friends, she took an available opportunity when they were both told to move some cattle out of a field. On the way, Hannah offered Jane some of the cake and Jane eagerly accepted.

The reports at the time state that she *'was soon after seized with dreadful pains and agonies'*. Whilst in excruciating pain she was attended to by her relatives and shortly before she died told them *'that the cake that she had eaten was the cause of the torment she suffered.'* Formal charges for the murder were laid on September 19, 1818.

In the early days after her arrest Hannah attempted to claim that several of her friends had been involved and even tried to implicate her sister, but this ploy failed. During the long imprisonment before her trial the Derby Mercury reported that *'she evinced no symptoms of contrition, but appeared more and more insensible as her inevitable fate drew near'*. Even the passing of the death sentence on her at her trial seemed to have virtually no effect on her disposition.

It was only as her date with the executioner drew near that she finally confessed, admitted her crime and added that she alone was solely responsible for it.

Hannah was executed on the New Drop outside the County Gaol on March 22, 1819. When she was 'launched into eternity' it was reported by the Derby Mercury that '*an involuntary shuddering pervaded the assembled crowd, and although she excited little sympathy, a general feeling of horror was expressed that one so young should have been so guilty, and so insensible*'.

The County Gaol on Friar Gate – site of the execution of Hannah Bocking – by Alfred John Keene.

Though her body was requested to be returned by friends for a burial, it was taken and dissected as per the law of the land.

It seems that although so young, her demeanour had offered Hannah little chance of a reprieve from the hangman's noose, though some people were lucky enough to receive them. You would assume that people who had so narrowly escaped a judicial death would perhaps change their ways, but only 11 days later a man who had so narrowly escaped the drop just two years previously, would, this time, get no such reprieve.

Thomas Hopkinson – a very temporary reprieve.

"Seldom seemed sufficiently impressed with the awful situation in which he himself was placed."

ACCOUNT OF THE LIFE, TRIAL & BEHAVIOUR OF
John Brown, Thomas Jackson, George Booth, & John King,
Who were Executed on the New Drop, in front of the County Gaol, Derby, on Friday August 15, 1817,
For Setting Fire to Hay and Corn Stacks.

The masthead of the broadside produced for the executions of John Brown, Thomas Jackson, George Booth and John King after the trial at which Thomas Hopkinson turned King's evidence.

It's an undeniable fact that some people seem to be naturally better at learning from their mistakes than others. Whilst certain people may find themselves to be doomed to repeat their errors time and time again, other sit back, take stock and learn a lesson. What often helps those more predisposed to learn is something that could be described as a shock or a jolt to the system, something that breeds a fear of ever being in that situation again. In 1817, Thomas Hopkinson was given such a shock – most would say an almighty one – but he appeared determined not to learn from it.

Born in Ashover, Thomas lived there until he was 14, after which the family moved to Wooley Moor. It was here that he would begin to fraternise with new companions with whom he would ultimately move into a life of crime. Amongst these were John Brown, Thomas Jackson, George Booth and John King.

It was with these other young men that, at the age of 18, he committed a crime that was a capital offence punishable by death – setting fire to hay and corn stacks. Corn was a very viable commodity since the implementation of the Corn Laws in 1815. These measures were a very emotive subject and acted to keep corn prices at a high level, with the intention of protecting English farmers from cheap foreign imports of grain following the end of the Napoleonic Wars. The system of crime and punishment we had in England at that time is now referred to as the *'Bloody Code'* - over 200 offences were punishable by death and this was very much one of them.

Whatever the motivation for Thomas and the other men was in destroying the corn of the owner of Wingfield Manor – Colonel Winfield Halton – is not conclusively known. What is known is that feelings were running high in the area in a fashion that would ultimately lead to the Pentrich uprising, but regardless of this the men were caught and tried.

Fearing that John King was about to betray the group, Thomas decided to move first and turned King's evidence, ensuring their demise and his safety.

What was notable about the execution was that minutes before it was due to take place a heavy rainstorm began and, as the Derby Mercury reported, *'two of them deliberately retreated to the shelter of an umbrella which was expanded on the drop, and a third placed himself under cover of the door way. The inconvenience of being wet was felt and avoided by men who knew that they had not five minutes longer to live!!'*

Undeterred by his brush with death, Thomas returned to his life of crime, robbing with impunity, until he was arrested in February 1819 for the crime of highway robbery. Whilst confined in prison, Thomas alternated from long periods of protesting his innocence to brief occasions where he admitted his guilt. Although stoic generally, he broke down on at least one occasion when he saw the condemned, 16-year-old Hannah Bocking, only an hour before her execution when she was in the prison chapel.

Thomas was executed on April 2, 1819. Thomas Jackson's father, having witnessed the execution of his son after Thomas Hopkinson had turned King's evidence two years prior, had volunteered to be the executioner. Whether this offer was accepted or not, is unknown. Though from an area, as we have previously mentioned, where unrest was common and where an uprising would occur, their executions meant they would play no part in any revolutionary fervour. Many others did though and three of them were hung and beheaded for it.

Pentrich Revolution – a levying of war against the King.

"Behold the Head of a Traitor."

Pentrich in Derbyshire.

Credit: Mike Bardill, CC BY-SA 2.0, via Wikimedia Commons.

When the Napoleonic Wars ended in 1816, the country was in a severe depression. Mass unemployment was rife due to the discharging of troops and the increasing industrialisation of workplaces. Alongside a poor harvest in 1817 and the Corn Laws creating severe increases in the price of bread, matters came to a head with the Pentrich Revolution.

For six years previously, there had been instances of local uprisings due to the employment of unskilled workers. It was amid this cauldron of discontent that a number of secret revolutionary committees were formed. The committee at Nottingham was led by a needle maker called William Stevens and the village of Pentrich was represented there by a framework knitter called Thomas Bacon.

Unbeknownst to these committees, in the spring the government had set up a series of spies and agent provocateurs to both inform them of any potential trouble, and also to create it, in order to clamp down and punish the ringleaders.

One of these agents – William Oliver – was responsible for fabricating a hoax that a large force of revolutionaries was marching down from the north of the country. The Nottingham committee aimed to join this hoax force on their supposed march to London in support of a bill by Sir Francis Burdett for parliamentary reform.

Thomas Bacon had a warrant out for his arrest at that time, so Jeremiah Brandreth was appointed to be his deputy and was in charge of getting them to Nottingham. On the way they wanted to invade the Butterley Ironworks so they could ransack it for weapons. Among the group of men were Isaac Ludlam, a bankrupted farmer and William Turner, an ex-soldier.

Around 50 men assembled at 10pm on June 9, 1817 at Hunt's Barn in South Wingfield. Over the next few hours they explored the local area for weapons and potential recruits, including at the house of the widow Mary Hepworth. Hepworth refused to open her doors to the men, which resulted in Jeremiah Brandreth firing a shot through a window which killed a servant.

When the men reached Butterley Ironworks their goal was thwarted by factory agent George Goodwin and a small group of constables who stood their ground and faced them down. With morale falling among the men, a few left the party and the remainder headed to Ripley. Although more men were pressed into service in Ripley, others defected and when they were met by a small force of soldiers in Giltbrook, they scattered. Around 40 were captured, and although the leaders escaped at the time, they were ultimately captured over the following weeks.

Twenty-three of the marchers were tried and sentenced for 'maliciously and traitorously [endeavouring]...by force of arms, to subvert and destroy the Government and the Constitution,' with three receiving a sentence of transportation for 14 years and 11 receiving a life sentence. The ring leaders were dealt with much more severely, however.

Thomas Bacon, Jeremiah Brandreth, Isaac Ludlam, William Turner and George Weightman were initially due to stand trial for high treason for which the sentence for a guilty verdict was death. Bacon, however, was now aware of the part that agent provocateur William Oliver had played in events, and to avoid him embarrassing the government with his testimony of this, Brandreth was tried as the leader alongside Ludlam, Turner and Weightman. All four were found guilty and received the sentence of the death penalty, although Weightman was reprieved due to a recommendation for leniency by the jury and received a sentence of transportation for life, alongside Bacon.

Sentenced to be hung, drawn and quartered, the Prince Regent commuted the drawing and quartering and the three men were to be hung until dead and then beheaded. On November 7,

1817 all three men were executed outside Derby Gaol with all three coffins buried in an unmarked grave at St. Werburgh's Church.

The thought of a sentence such as hanging, drawing and quartering is something that our modern day minds would find repulsive, however, surely if any sentence would make us even more likely to be repulsed it is being burned at the stake. That was the tragic and horrific fate that befell a 22-year-old blind woman in Derby in 1556.

Her crime? Her religion.

Joan Waste - a Reformation Martyr.

"Are you prepared to die for your doctrine?"

Joan Waste was born blind in 1534 to Derby barber William Waste and his wife Joan. Despite being blind it is noted that by the age of 12 Joan had learnt to knit well and how to make rope – a skill she had picked up from her father who, alongside barbering, also made rope.

A devout Christian, Joan attended mass regularly at St. Peter's Church in Derby and was herself a Protestant - a form of Christianity that originated with the 16th-century Reformation, a movement against what its followers perceived to be errors in the Catholic Church. This, at first, would have been of no concern to anyone until when, in 1555, when Joan was 21, Queen Mary I, who had ascended the throne in 1553, made it illegal by Parliament to hold Protestant views. Anyone who disobeyed this was accused of heresy which was punishable by death.

Joan's devout and Protestant nature was well known in the town. From an early age she had taken it upon herself to visit Derby gaols and it was in the debtor's prison that she befriended an elderly man in his 70s – John Hurt. John would regularly read her passages from the bible she owned, as would other like-minded people. With Joan steadfast in her Protestant beliefs such as her refusal to accept the doctrine of transubstantiation - the belief in the conversion of the communion bread and wine into the body and blood of Christ at consecration - maintaining they were still bread and wine and merely symbolic, it was inevitable that a clash would occur with the authorities.

Joan was called to answer the charges against her and faced the Diocesan Bishop, Ralph Baine and his Chancellor, Dr Anthony Draycott. The march of time, when it turns and looks back on itself, has been unkind to the Chancellor, and rightfully so. His reign as Chancellor involved condemning numerous people needlessly to their premature death.

Her trial took place at what was then All Saints Parish Church – now Derby Cathedral – and answering her charges she made it abundantly clear that she was aware of a number of people that had been imprisoned, tortured and killed for their beliefs. She said:

"Are you prepared to die for your doctrine? If not, then for God's sake trouble me no more. I am but a poor, blind, uneducated woman, but with God's help I am ready to yield up my life in this faith."

Staying steadfast throughout her trial she was remanded to the bailiffs in Derby and placed in prison where she received the news that she would be burnt as a heretic. The sentence of being burnt at the stake, involved the strangulation of the victim before the fire was lit, but on many occasions, this proved to be ineffective and the victim would come around, only for the flames to burn through the ropes causing them to fall into the flames and die in agony.

Joan and her family attended services at St Peter's in Derby where they heard the services in English until Mary became Queen.
Credit: Jerry Evans / St Peter's Church, Derby

No record of whether this happened to Joan exists, or at least has never been uncovered, but what is known is that her last day on this earth was August 1, 1556. On that day she was taken to church where Dr Anthony Draycott himself gave a sermon. Afterwards – and while Draycott himself merely went to his abode to eat – she was taken to Windmill Hill Pit, which lies just off the modern-day Burton Road in Derby, where the sentence was carried out.

Of all the punishments meted out during the area's history, this must surely be one of the most undeserved and brutal.

Joan was sadly not the only person to be executed in Derby for their faith. Three priests were executed in 1588 for their beliefs – only this time they were executed because they were Roman Catholics.

The Padley Martyrs – brutality unbridled.

"Dragged on hurdles to their place of execution."

Whereas the reign of Queen Mary I had seen the persecution of Protestants, when she died in 1558 and Queen Elizabeth I came to the throne, the kingdom shifted over to Protestantism.

Though initially more lenient than Mary when it came to religious differences, Catholics still had cause to be wary and could find themselves being treated unfairly and with harshness. As time went on, the anti-Catholic sentiment in the kingdom grew stronger and when the Babington Plot – a plot to overthrow Elizabeth and replace her with Mary, Queen of Scots – was uncovered in 1586, emotions ran higher still. Two years later, in 1588, with the imminent attack of the Spanish Armada being planned, emotions reached fever pitch.

It was in this environment that three Catholic priests - Nicholas Garlick, Robert Ludlam and Richard Simpson met their end.

Across the kingdom the authorities searched for Catholic recusants – Catholics who were refusing to submit and obey the law of the land at that time and who were secretly organising and celebrating Catholic mass. When the Earl of Shrewsbury and Lord Lieutenant of Derbyshire, led a speculative raid for this reason on Padley Hall near Hathersage on July 12, 1588, he captured and arrested John Fitzherbert – the head of a known and established Catholic family and two Catholic priests – Father Nicholas Garlick and Father Robert Ludlam. The three prisoners were escorted firstly to Sheffield Castle and then on to the gaol in Derby.

Whilst in gaol awaiting their trial they encountered a third priest – Father Richard Simpson. Simpson had been sentenced to death earlier that year, but for reasons unknown had been given a temporary delay in his execution. Ultimately on July 23 all three men would be sentenced to death by one of the most brutal methods – hanging, drawing and quartering. Fitzherbert was also sentenced to die, but he was spared.

If someone was to suffer this fate, they would be hanged, but only until they were almost at the point of death. They would then, while still alive, have their penis and testicles removed and then be disembowelled. Following this they would be beheaded and their body was then cut into four pieces or as it was called – quartered.

This grisly and undeserved act happened in Derby on St. Mary's Bridge on July 24, 1588 after the prisoners had been dragged on hurdles by horses to their place of execution.

St. Mary s Bridge in Derby.

Credit: David Hallam-Jones / Derby - St Mary's Bridge

After their barbaric execution, the mutilated remains of the unfortunate men were placed on poles and displayed in various places as a warning to others.

Since 1898, an annual pilgrimage to Padley has taken place in honour of the martyrs, though many people still travel over the bridge unaware of the area's gruesome past.

As with any execution a crowd gathered to watch, though nowhere near the crowd that gathered for the execution of Samuel Bonsall, William Bland and John Hulme which attracted a reputed crowd of over 40,000 people.

Bonsall, Bland and Hulme – killing as entertainment.

"The crowd, as seen from the scaffold, presented a densely packed mass of human beings..."

The façade of Vernon Street Gaol, or prison – site of the execution of Bonsall, Bland and Hulme - still stands today.

Credit: James Haynes / Vernon Gate, Derby

Over the years, many large crowds have gathered for a variety of reasons in Derby, whether that be for celebratory reasons such as VE Day or sporting events such as following our football team – Derby County Football Club. Indeed the record home attendance for 'The Rams' occurred in 1969 at a home game against Spurs and was 41,826. Most people may not be aware that this attendance was, according to reports of the time, matched, if not exceeded, by an execution in Derby 126 years earlier.

The masses had come to witness the execution of three men - Samuel Bonsall, William Bland and John Hulme – all sentenced to hang for the brutal murder of Miss Martha Goddard, an elderly woman who, in 1842, lived with her sister Sarah.

Martha had been murdered during a burglary by the three men on September 30 of that year with a reward immediately offered for any information that would lead to the conviction of the perpetrators. The Derby Mercury newspaper publicised the reward in their edition of October 5 as follows:

"Whereas the dwelling-house of the two Misses Goddard, at Stanley, in the county of Derby, was burglariously broken into, and entered early in the morning of the 30th day of September, and both of the inmates inhumanly beat about their heads and faces, one of whom has since died from the wounds inflicted;-Notice is hereby given, that a reward of £100, will be given to any person who shall give such information as will lead to the conviction of the perpetrators of the above crime, on application to Mr. R. W. Birch, solicitor, Derby."

Bonsall, Bland and Hulme were all regular burglars and all prone to violence as part of their methods. Bonsall and Bland both hailed from Heage, while Hulme, who had seen two of his brothers transported for their criminal activities, was from Leek.

The murder weapon the men had used was a crowbar and it was William Bland who struck the murderous blows, three all told. At the inquest, the deceased's sister told the coroner:

"…the deceased, Martha Goddard, was my sister; she was about 69 years of age, and unmarried; she and I lived together, we kept no servant; on Thursday night last, my sister went to bed about 10 o'clock; I sat up a great deal later; about half-past twelve o'clock on Friday morning I was sitting by the fire in the house-place and heard a noise like mortar falling, the sound came from the coal-house, the door of which was open, and just as I got to it there came out of it two men, who knocked me down, and afterwards went up to my sister's room; when I was able to get up again I went up stairs to my room, and the men came into it and knocked me down again with heavy iron bars; they beat me very much about the head and hands, and broke one of my fingers; I have no doubt they killed my sister with the iron bars they had in their hands, they were very stern savage men, they stayed in the house about an hour and a half, and they then left it; soon after they had gone I went into my sister's room and found her lying bleeding, on her back across the bed, with her legs lying down; I put her legs on a chair, and stayed with her till about 5 o'clock, when I went out and alarmed the neighbours…"

By October 12, 1842 the Derby Mercury was already reporting that the suspects had been apprehended and on March 20, 1843 the three men stood trial and were all found guilty. Bland confessed to being the one to strike the killing blows and they were all sentenced to death by hanging.

The execution took place shortly after the trial on March 31. For reasons unknown, the decision had been made to build the scaffolding for the drop to the left of the top of the gaol's main gateway, offering much greater viewing opportunities for those eager to witness the executions.

People poured into the town from places such as Belper and Chesterfield on specially laid on trains organised by the North Midland Railway and Derby was described by the Derby Mercury as:

"...inundated by thousands of persons from the neighbouring villages, and from a considerable distance, to witness their ignominious exit. The number assembled up to the time of execution could not be less than 35,000 to 40,000."

Other contemporary reports described the crowd as high as 50,000. Although executions were indeed a popular viewing activity, that was an unusually large crowd, even by the standards of the time.

The execution of George Ashmore would have had a substantially smaller number of attendees, but for George there would be no rest for his remains as, after his execution, feared Resurrection men paid his grave a visit.

George Ashmore – the Resurrection men.

"In no case whatsoever shall the body of any murderer be suffered to be buried."

When researching numerous crimes, most of them involving murder, it's not uncommon to become if not numb, at least accustomed to reading the barbaric details of the crimes themselves and executions that followed them. From time to time though something stands out from the literature, and in the case of George Ashmore in 1740, it was the appearance of the Resurrection men or body-snatchers.

Like our earlier friend Noah Bullock, George was a counterfeiter. George, alongside all the other members of his illicit trade, was aware that if caught he would face the ultimate penalty, but George had already come closer than a lot of others to doing just that.

Just a year before his ultimate demise, George had turned King's evidence against another counterfeiter – George Brentnal – in an act of self-preservation that, whilst sparing him in the moment, ultimately had no bearing on him mending his ways or altering his path.

George was soon enough arrested again and on August 29, 1740 he was executed. The day after his execution the lifeless body was claimed by relatives and taken to Sutton-on-the-Hill for burial.

St Michael's Church, Sutton-on-the-Hill.

Credit: Geoff Pick / St. Michael, Sutton-on-the-Hill

At that time in our history, corpses were a highly sought-after commodity – they were quite understandably needed by medical professionals for dissection in an attempt to learn more about the human body, but demand outstripped supply.

The Murder Act (1752), aimed to help with this when, with its peculiar dual intent of combining the procurement of corpses, with the element of *'post-mortem punishment'* decreed that *'in no case whatsoever shall the body of any murderer be suffered to be buried'*, stating the bodies should either be dissected or hung in chains. Demand still outstripped supply then – and George's execution was 12 years prior to the act becoming law.

Though precautions were often taken to try to ensure that the bodies were left in peace the Resurrection men would still, on many occasions, manage to exhume a corpse for financial gain. Within a couple of days of his burial this was the fate that the body of George Ashmore would suffer. Observant villagers in Sutton-on-the-Hill noticed that the ground around the grave had been disturbed and feared the worst. When the grave was dug up it was discovered that his coffin and the shroud George had been buried in were still there – but the body was gone.

Through other researchers before me, the lives and deaths of people such as George Ashmore have been recorded for posterity, even though at the time of their demise this would only have been relatively minor news.

Others, however, managed to cause quite a stir in their own time, such as George Smith, the perpetrator of patricide whose crime drew national headlines and a crowd bigger than the one that witnessed the executions of Samuel Bonsall, William Bland and John Hulme.

George Smith – the Ilkeston patricide.

"Here's heart that ne'er will fail; To swing under the gallows or under a rail."

In the Victorian language of the time, George Smith was what would have been referred to as a *'rake'* – a man for whom immoral conduct was common, particularly in the case of womanising.

The eldest son of Joseph and Harriett, George was 20-years-old when he found himself standing in front of the Derby Assizes, facing a packed courtroom on July 29, 1861 where he was accused of the murder of his own father. George was a twist-hand (lace maker) by trade and his father Joseph had been a shoemaker who resided on Bath Street in Ilkeston and was described at that time as *'a man of property'*. It was a combination of George's womanising and his anger at what he perceived as a lack of financial support from his family, plus the tinderbox of heavy drinking that all contributed to the horrific charge that George was facing.

Earlier that year one of the many ladies that George frequently spent time with, told him that she was pregnant with his baby. Though it seems that there was no dispute, even from George himself, that he was indeed the father, it also seems that he had no intention of paying any form of maintenance for the new life he had helped create.

George's friends, enlisted by him, tried to persuade the lady in question to drop the claim but this proved unsuccessful. On learning this news, George hatched his next plan which was to move to France to avoid any question of paying anything. His desire to avoid paying any money evidently didn't match his actual desire to move to France.

When he had made it as far as Leicestershire, he stayed there for two days and then promptly returned to Ilkeston.

Throughout all this George was drinking heavily and nursing a burning hatred and resentment towards his father who he felt should have helped him financially. George's father quite probably, and rightly, thought that George needed to first deal with his own self-inflicted problems and it was on May 1 that all of this came to a gruesome conclusion.

George had very recently purchased a pistol, powder and caps from a shop in Nottingham and, on his return to Ilkeston, he purchased a pennyworth of shot. On May 1, he went to his father's house and found him asleep on the sofa. Walking to the bottom of the garden, he loaded the pistol before returning to the house with the premeditated intent of committing murder. By the time he had walked back inside the house his father was no longer there. Heading to a public house, George got drunk and convinced himself not to kill his father. Heading back to the house, to which his father still had not returned, George placed the pistol in a drawer and returned to the public house for more drinking.

By the time George returned to the house once more he was very drunk and agitated. An argument ensued and, pulling the pistol back out of the drawer, George shot his father dead. Upon his arrest a drunken George sang lines he had heard during visits to the theatre:

"Here's heart that ne'er will fail; To swing under the gallows or under a rail."

Faced with overwhelming evidence, George Smith was soon convicted and sentenced to hang on August 16.

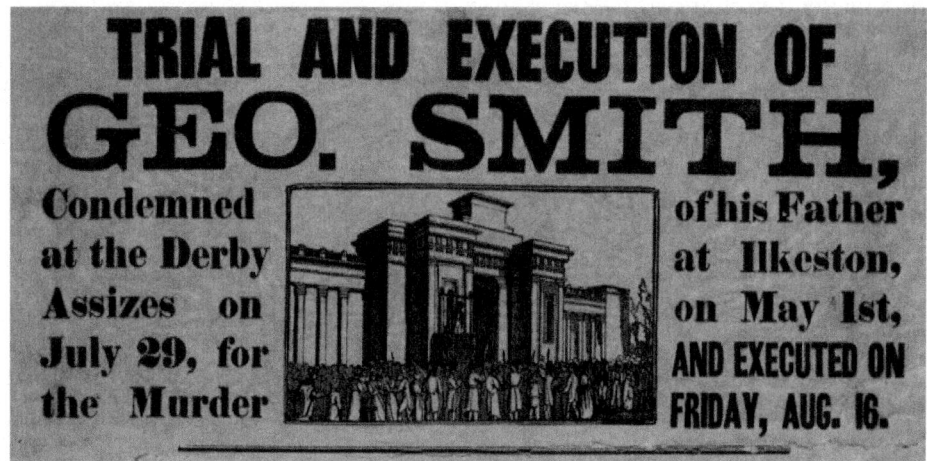

The masthead of the broadside produced for the execution of George Smith.

Special trains were laid on once more and estimates at the time suggested as many as 50,000 people turned up to see the first public execution in nine years.

Notably the Derby Mercury stated in its August 21, 1861 edition:

"It is useless to dilate with a morbid minuteness upon the performance of the hangman's duties, but the shrieks and sobs which rose in a few minutes after Smith got up told the man who turned sickened from the sight that all was over."

All in all, George Smith took around ten minutes to die as he was slowly strangled to death.

On the day of their execution, each and every person would, of course, behave differently. Some would face their fate with a stern resolve and others not so. George Smith was reported to have *'walked with a firm step from the Chaplain's room to the scaffold'*. Others, such as John and Benjamin Jones, were determined to avoid the hangman at any cost, including taking their own lives.

John and Benjamin Jones – the ultimate escape.

"The two Criminals presented an awful sight, which made him retreat and call for help."

It's hard to comprehend what would go through the mind of a person who is held in custody awaiting their own execution. In bygone times, and as we can see from our other prisoners, there was no extended time period full of appeals between the passing of the death sentence and the actual execution.

In the case of two brothers – John and Benjamin Jones – the knowledge of their impending fate pushed them into taking the only way out that they had, suicide, within a day of the sentence being passed – and as had happened in many cases, an informant played a part.

According to the evidence of the informant, both brothers were career criminals. When they stood before the judge at the Derby Assizes on August 3, 1784, it was to face a long list of charges.

Amongst the crimes they lay accused of committing with the informant, were: a burglary committed by John and the informant at the house of widows at Nuns Green; a burglary with both brothers and the informant in the village of Culland, near Brailsford; a further burglary in Ashbourne on March 28, 1784; another burglary in Culland; a burglary without Benjamin present at a warehouse near St. Peter's Church in Derby and a burglary at the house of a Mrs. Roe in St. Peter's Parish.

With such a long list of charges as well as the evidence of the informant, it is of no surprise that a guilty verdict was returned, and their date of execution was set for August 20.

The brothers were returned back to the gaol at Friar Gate and were initially full of bravado despite their impending doom. It was a level of bravado which dissipated once they were placed back into a cell, with John in particular, becoming very distressed.

As there were only the two of them in the cell it's impossible to know exactly what was discussed, but it seems that there was agreement from both men that it would be better to die from their own hands, than from those of the hangman.

It was a turnkey who discovered them the next day. Wearing only their shirts, both men were found hanging from the cord used to secure their chains, which they had tied to a mortice hole above the door of their cell. The turnkey called for help and a surgeon arrived. The surgeon bled the men in an attempt to save them, presumably so they could still be executed, but was unsuccessful – the men were clearly already dead.

The last remaining cells of the Friar Gate Goal – now a museum.

Contemporary documents which told the story of the men hoped that:

"The Fate of these Men may be a Warning to Youth, to shun those Paths of Vice."

However, history shows us that it wasn't.

If the intent of the brothers was to avoid the gallows entirely, then they were not completely successful, because later that afternoon their bodies were buried beneath it.

As hysterical as John might have been, we've seen that the law itself was known for its own hysteria on many occasions. It was in 1596 that this hysteria reared its ugly head when a woman was accused of being a witch. Like John and Benjamin she escaped the hangman, although it was not through suicide

Alice Gooderidge – a death caused by ignorance.

"Gyp with a mischief, and fart with a bell. I will go to Heaven, and you will go to Hell."

Convicted on the false testimony of a 14-year-old boy – Thomas Darling – Alice was very much a victim of the hysteria of the time. In many ways Alice didn't fit the stereotype of what a supposed witch was – she was married, held relatively large land holdings and had family living locally in Burton – although contemporary reports state that she suffered from facial warts and perhaps in these barbarically simple times, this alongside a false testimony, was enough to convince a hysterical judiciary of her guilt.

It was on February 17,1596 that the fateful encounter between Thomas and Alice would occur. Thomas was hunting alongside his uncle in Winsall Wood, less than a mile from Burton, and when separated from his uncle during the hunt, decided to make his own way home. Passing Alice, and quite probably due to some teenage mischief, he broke wind as he did. Alice was alleged to have responded with the words:

"Gyp with a mischief, and fart with a bell. I will go to Heaven, and you will go to Hell."

A short while later, Thomas began to suffer from a series of 'fits'. These fits lasted for several months and Thomas told of visions he saw during them, including seeing the flames of hell.

Elizabeth Toone, his aunt, called during this time for a local doctor, who finding nothing amiss, suggested bewitchment. Unconvinced, and suspecting epilepsy, she summoned a local folk-healer, Jesse Bee, who concurred with the diagnosis of bewitchment and prescribed the treatment of sitting with the boy and reading from the Gospel of St John. It wasn't long before Thomas began to tell the story of his encounter with Alice and soon the idea of demonic possession had taken hold.

When Alice was brought to the Darlings' house, Thomas promptly threw another fit and within two days both Alice and her mother were arrested. Both of them were not only questioned but also subjected to intimate examinations and alleged 'witch marks' were found on Alice. Though her mother was released, Alice was placed in a cell in the Derby Gaol.

It was in gaol that Alice made a forced confession. In her confession she said she had placed a spell on Thomas because of his rudeness and said she had sent a familiar spirit, a red and white dog called Minny, to torment him. It seemed irrelevant to the authorities that this confession was made by making Alice wear new shoes before putting her feet near a hot fireplace until, seeking relief from the unbearable heat, she confessed. Taken to Burton for more questioning, she was in the presence of Thomas again when this time he, rather predictably, he began to fit again. All in all he had 37 successive fits until Alice responded with one of her own and refused to talk any further.

Arraigned before Sir Edmund Anderson, a known believer in the dangers of witchcraft and witches, Alice was found guilty and returned to the gaol to await the hangman.

Sir Edmund Anderson.

Like both John and Benjamin Jones though, the hangman did not get his chance to earn his pay. Pestilence was rife in the gaol at the time and a few days before she was due to be hanged, Alice passed away.

The case of Alice Gooderidge is another tragic example of someone who fell foul of the persecution of so-called 'witches' around that time. 178 years later, a man would commit a genuine and brutal crime and flee all the way to Ireland to try to evade justice, before becoming the last man to be gibbeted in Derby.

Matthew Cocklayne – the last Derby gibbeting.

"A Mitigation of punishment would be an offence against the Laws of God himself."

Full Street c.1760 by S. H. Parkins.

Born in Ireland, Matthew Cocklayne had, for several years, been a solder in the Thirty-third Regiment of Foot. Upon his discharge, he had moved to Derby where he worked in the Copper Mills, and it would be on Full Street, Derby, where he would commit the act that ultimately led to his execution.

Though his army record was unblemished, once in Derby he became associated with a man called George Foster and together they began a career of petty theft.

It was on December 18, 1774, that the two men decided to rob the house of Mary Vickers, who lived with a servant girl. After breaking into the house, the men headed upstairs and she awakened as they entered her room. As she jumped out of bed to challenge them, Cocklayne beat her with an iron bar. While Foster pinned her down, and according to Cocklayne, also pushed a handkerchief into her mouth to stop her screaming, he broke open a chest in the room and stole around £300 – rather a large sum of money at the time. Various rings were also stolen.

Unfortunately for the men, the noise had alerted the servant girl who saw the men as they made their escape. Cocklayne threatened the girl as they exited the property and fled along Full Street, perhaps sure in his mind that the threats would be enough to keep her quiet as to their identities.

Mrs Vickers succumbed to the injuries she had sustained, and a broadside produced at the time described the scene of the crime in brutal terms, though it must be said that many of these documents were deliberately salacious. Nevertheless, it stated:

"Her Head was almost cut off, and her Scull was so terribly fractured that on moving her the Brains appeared."

Cocklayne and Foster had agreed to split up and meet again at a tavern in Liverpool. It was whilst they were here that the men discovered that they were now wanted for both murder and robbery. Terrified, as no doubt their poor victim had been, the men made their way to the docks and boarded a ferry to Dublin.

Resuming their criminal career in Ireland, their fugitive lives ended when, during a robbery, Foster was shot in the head, dying three days later, and Cocklayne was captured. Upon his capture it was found out that he was wanted in Derby, and he was returned there to stand trial where he was found guilty and sentenced to death by hanging. Key to the guilty verdict was the servant girl recognising his voice.

On March 21, 1776 the sentence was carried out. The judge, Sir Henry Ashurt, had added dissection to the sentence, though after a request from the family of Mrs. Vickers, this was altered to Matthew's dead body being gibbeted. The request was granted, and the remains were indeed gibbeted at Bradshaw Hay – near to the present-day Bradshaw Way.

His corpse was to hang there for many years. In 1791, fifteen years after it had first been gibbeted, the Derby Mercury reported that:

"A lad was met coming into this town, having in his hand the skull of Matthew Cocklane, who was executed on the 21st of March, 1776, for the murder of Mrs. Vickars, and afterwards hung in chains: It seems that the wind had blown him from his exalted situation the preceding night. His hair, skin, and most of his bones were in high preservation; numbers – who had often stood in melancholy gaze, repaired to the gibbet, and returned with various parts of his remains."

That his remains were so well preserved is a testament to the preserving tar that was used on gibbeted corpses. But as times moved on, and the practice of gibbeting ceased, many corpses were dealt with in a cursory fashion after the execution.

This was certainly the case with William Slack, the last person to be executed in Derby in 1907.

William Slack – Derby's last execution.

No hope of a reprieve is entertained."

By the time 1907 had rolled around, executions in Derby and Derbyshire had been occurring for at least 600 years. By 1907, outside of military law, only five offences were now capital offences - murder, treason, espionage, arson in royal dockyards, and piracy with violence.

It will probably come as no surprise that it was the first of these that William Slack was accused and found guilty of.

William was 47-years-old and a painter by trade, but even before the murder he was accused of, he had gained the reputation of being a violent man. Previously he had been found guilty of attempting to murder a police constable and had served seven years of hard labour for the attempt. His first wife had also left him – unable to cope with his violent outbursts.

No longer answerable to his first wife, William had embarked upon an affair with a married 40-year-old barmaid – Lucy Wilson – in Chesterfield. Shortly before Lucy herself broke up with William, she had given birth to a son – quite possibly William's son.

Chesterfield – location of the murder of Lucy Wilson by William Slack.
jondaniel, CC BY 3.0 via Wikimedia Commons

It was whilst walking her son in his pram, that she bumped into William on Highfield Road in Chesterfield.

The two of them became embroiled in a heated argument until William, absurdly claiming provocation, took out a hatchet and struck the fatal blows – all in front of the young baby boy.

Though he went on to escape, pushing the boy in his pram with him, he was pursued by a postman who had witnessed the entire event. The postman managed to persuade William to stop running and give himself up.

Though not denying that he had killed Lucy with his hatchet, William argued that he had been provoked and should not hang for it and pleaded not guilty to the charge of murder.

Despite his pleas, he was found guilty and sentenced to hang – the date was set for July 16, 1907

Reports at the time said that when the judge reached for his black cap, shortly before passing the death sentence, William, *"Made use of an offensive expression, used filthy and violent language and refused to face the Bench while the death sentence was being carried out, struggling with the wardens meanwhile."*

On the day of his execution, he was taken to the shed inside the gaol where executions now took place. His grave - ready and waiting for him - was facing the doors of his shed.

The executioner was Henry Pierrepoint - the most senior executioner in the country – and the execution went without a hitch.

Unlike the likes of Matthew Cocklayne and Anthony Lingard, whose corpses were gibbeted; the Padley Martyrs, whose mutilated remains were displayed on poles; the ringleaders of the Pentrich Revolution, whose corpses were beheaded; George Ashmore, whose remains were stolen by the Resurrection men; or the many others who were dissected, the earthly remains of William Slack were dealt with quickly and summarily as his corpse was covered in quicklime and buried without ceremony. This also brought to an end the era of executions in Derby and Derbyshire which died alongside him.

A list of all the known executions in Derbyshire.

1341

A woman and two men were hanged and gibbeted for murdering one of the King's purveyors at Ashover Moor.

1341

The bodies of three men were hung in chains at Chapel-en-le-Frith for robbery with violence.

c.16th century

On the orders of Sir George Vernon an unidentified pedlar was hanged at Ashford-in-the-Water.

1556

On August 1, Joan Waste was burnt at the stake as a heretic at Windmill Hill Pit. Windmill Hill Pit is on Lime Avenue which is just off Burton Road in Derby.

1578

Peter Graves of Bubnall, Thomas Robinson of Wirksworth, Eleanor Wright of Bakewell, Edward Morrys of Chesterfield and Christopher Harrison of Monyash were hanged at Derby.

1588

On July 24 three Catholic priests, Nicholas Garlick, Robert Ludlam and Richard Simpson, were hanged, drawn and quartered for high treason on St. Mary's Bridge in Derby.

1591

Seven unknown persons were hanged at Derby.

1599

A man named Okey was hanged in the Town Hall in Derby.

1601

A woman was burnt at Windmill Pit, Derby, for poisoning her husband.

c.1607/08

Mrs. Stafford and another female were executed for witchcraft.

1608

Five men and one woman were hanged at Tapton Bridge, the Assizes having been held at Chesterfield owing to the prevalence of the plague in Derby.

1608

Henry Bennett was hanged at Derby for the murder of Roger Moore, a serjeant. It is said that his mother and brother were also involved in the murder.

1645

Richard Cockrum was hanged at the gallows in Nun's Green for killing a girl named Mills, a servant at the Angel Inn, in the Cornmarket, Derby.

c.1660

John Crossland and his eldest son were hanged for horse stealing. The hangman was John Jr - his youngest son, who then took on the job of official hangman.

1665

On March 14, a woman was pressed to death in the County Hall in Derby. This was the last instance of someone receiving this punishment in England.

1679

Ten members of The Bracy Gang were executed for highway robbery.

1693

A girl in farm service at Swanick was burnt for murdering her master. This was the last case in Derbyshire of death by burning at the stake.

1723

A man was hanged at Derby for horse stealing.

1725

Three men, (Rock, Lyon and Shaw), were hanged at Derby for counterfeit coining.

1726

A man was hanged at Derby for horse stealing.

1727

A man was hanged at Derby for horse stealing.

1732

On March 29, John Hewitt and Rosamund Ollerenshaw were hanged for poisoning Hannah Hewitt at the Crown Inn in Nun's Green, Derby.

1735

On August 15, John Smith was hanged in Derby for burglary after breaking into the house of Mr Bowyer of Roston and stealing a silver cup.

1738

On March 30, Richard Woodward was hanged at Derby for highway robbery.

1740

On April 9, William Dolphin was hanged at Derby for the highway robbery of a Mr. Lord near Chesterfield.

1740

On August 29, George Ashmore was hanged for coining. After the execution he was buried at Sutton-on-the-Hill. The body was removed the next day by body snatchers.

1741

On April 10, 1741 William Elliott was hanged for stealing.

1741

On August 7, Robert Bowler was hanged for shooting at Edward Rivington on the highway between Belper and Pentrich.

1754

On March 23, Mary Dilkes was hanged for the murder of her child on January 1.

1755

On August 1, Ann Williamson was hanged for picking the pocket of George White of six guineas and a Portuguese gold coin (valued at 36/-) at Ashbourne Fair.

1756

On April 2, John Ratcliffe was hanged for horse stealing.

1757

On April 29, Thomas Hulley was hanged for being at large in the Kingdom (i.e., returning from transportation) on Friday April 29, 1757.

1759

On March 24, Charles Kirkman was hanged for the murder of his illegitimate child and dissected in accordance with Murder Act of 1752.

1763

On August 12, James Perry and Amos Mason were hanged for highway robbery of a Mr Staveley.

1768

On April 20, John Low was hanged for housebreaking.

1768

On May 4, Charles Pleasants was hanged for forgery.

1776

On March 21, Matthew Cocklane was hanged and gibbeted for the murder of Mary Vickers during the course of a burglary at her house on Sunday December 18, 1774, when he stole £300 in money and rings. He was the last person to be gibbeted in Derby.

1780

On March 31, James Meadows, 30, from Handsworth near Birmingham, was hanged for highway robbery. He had robbed William Featherstone of £40 at Gag Lane near Tissington on Sunday October 31, 1779.

1780

On August 25, William Buxton, 26, was hanged for highway robbery. Buxton had been convicted of robbing John Kennedy of six Guineas in gold, some silver and also another highway robbery on July 20, between Buxton and Ashbourne.

1782

On March 28, James Williams was hanged for stealing a dark brown gelding (horse) valued at £15.15s, the property of Mr Worthington of Altrincham.

1782

On August 2, John Shaw was hanged for being at large, having broken out of Derby Gaol to avoid transportation.

1784

On April 8, Thomas Greensmith was executed for a burglary in the premises of Messrs. Rea and Co. watchmakers of Walton-on-Trent.

1784

On April 16, William Rose was hanged for horse stealing.

1785

On April 1, William and George Grooby and James Peat were hanged for burglary at the shop of Samuel Leam of Pentrich.

1786

On April 7, John Shepherd, 49, was executed for breaking into the house of Mr Smith at Sandiacre and stealing therefrom. With him on the gallows was William Stanley, 25, who had been convicted of breaking into the house of Thomas Parker at Winshill.

1786

On September 2, James Halliburton was hanged for the rape of Millicent Smith of Biggin.

1787

On April 9, John Porson was hanged for picking the pocket of John Johnson of eight gold guineas and 11 silver shillings.

1788

On March 22, Thomas Grundy was hanged and dissected for poisoning his brother at Dale-Abbey in 1787.

1790

On August 12, Joseph Allen was hanged for stealing two silver candlesticks from the premises of Thomas Barker of Derby.

1791

On April 1, William Rider was hanged for the rape of Mary Barton near Mackeney toll bar and robbing her of three pence.

1794

On April 4, James Murray was hanged for house breaking. He had broken into the house of Mr Farnworth at Codnor Park in November 1793.

1795

On April 10, Thomas Neville was hanged for the highway robbery of John Morley on January 2, the same year; robbing him of 14½ gold guineas and some silver.

1796

On March 17, James Preston, 70, was hanged for the murder of Susannah Moreton's illegitimate child. Susannah Moreton was also condemned for this murder but was reprieved on the morning of the execution.

1800

On September 5, Thomas Knowles was executed for uttering a forged guinea note with intent to defraud.

1801

On August 14, a quintuple hanging occurred when John Dent, 47, was hanged for the theft of two cows, the property of Mr Creswell of Ravenstone; John Evans, 22, was hanged for stealing two sacks of oats from a barn; Lacy Powell, 23, and John Drummond, 26, were hanged for a highway robbery and James Gration, 25, was hanged for a burglary in the house of Philip Yeomans of Shuttle in March 1801, stealing eight gold guineas, seven shillings and other goods.

1802

On August 27, James Mellor and Thomas Spencer were executed. James was executed for the theft of a pony and Thomas was hanged for burglary in the house of Mr Flint of Biggin.

1803

On March 19, William Wells was hanged for murder. His body was afterwards dissected in the Shire Hall in St. Mary's Gate.

1804

On April 6, Richard Boothe and John Parker were hanged for horse stealing.

1807

On March 20, William Webster, 34, was hanged for poisoning Thomas Dakin, Elizabeth Dakin and Mary Roe, in the parish of Hartington.

1807

On April 3, Joseph West was hanged for forgery. He was the last person to be hanged at Nuns Green.

1812

On April 10, James Tomlinson, 27, and Percival Cook, 26, were hanged on the New Drop in front of the county gaol in Friar Gate for breaking into Mr Hunt's house in Ockbrook.

1813

On April 9, Paul Mason, 34, Richard Hibbert, 24, and Peter Henshaw, 40, were hanged for burglary.

1815

On March 28, Anthony Lingard, 21, from Litton, was hanged and gibbeted for the murder of Hannah Oliver, keeper of the Turnpike Gate at Wardlow Mires. This was the last gibbeting to take place in Derbyshire.

1816

On August 9, Joseph Wheeldon was executed and afterwards dissected in Derby for the murders of his niece, Mary Ann Wheeldon and nephew, Isaac Wheeldon.

1817

On August 15, John Brown, Thomas Jackson, George Boothe and John King were hanged for setting fire to hay and corn stacks in South Wingfield.

1817

On November 7, Jeremiah Brandreth, William Turner and Isaac Ludlam, (The Pentrich Martyrs) were hanged and beheaded for high treason.

1819

On March 22, Hannah Bocking, 16, was hanged for poisoning Jane Grant at Wardlow Miers, within sight of the gibbet containing Anthony Lingard's bones.

1819

On April 2, Thomas Hopkinson was hanged for highway robbery. Hopkinson had been tried with John Brown, Thomas Jackson, George Boothe and John King but had turned King's evidence.

1822

On March 25, Hannah Halley of Brook Street, Derby, was hanged for murdering her infant child. She was the last woman to be hanged in Derby and the last to be dissected.

1825

On April 8, George Batty was hanged for the rape of 16-year-old Martha Hawksley. This was the last execution carried out at the county gaol in Friar Gate.

1833

On April 12, John Leedham was hanged for bestiality with a sheep. This was the first execution to take place in front of the new county gaol in Vernon Street, and he was the last person to hang in Derbyshire for a crime other than murder.

1843

On March 31, Samuel Bonsall, William Bland and John Hulme, (alias Holmes, alias Starbuck, alias Jack the Sweep) were hanged for the murder of Martha Goddard. The execution took place from the top of the gatehouse in the county gaol of Vernon Street.

1847

On April 1, 22-year-old John Platts was hanged by Samuel Haywood atop the gatehouse of the county gaol for the murder of George Collis at Brampton. He died hard, struggling for two minutes, according to newspaper reports. The crowd that turned out for his execution was estimated to be around 20,000.

1852

On March 23, Anthony Turner was hanged for the murder of Phoebe Barnes at Belper. Phoebe had previously dismissed him from his job as a rent collector after which he then got drunk and murdered her with a carving knife. He was hanged in Belper.

1861

On August 16, George Smith, 20, was hanged for the murder of his father in Ilkeston.

1862

On April 11, Richard Thorley was hanged for the murder of Eliza Morrow in Agard Street, Derby. This was the last public execution held in Derby.

1873

On August 4, Benjamin Hudson was hanged for the murder of his wife Eliza during an argument at West Handley on April 24.

1880

On August 16, John Wakefield was hanged for the murder of nine-year-old Elizabeth Wilkinson. His motive was apparently suicide by judicial hanging.

1881

On February 28, Albert Robinson was hanged for the murder of his wife.

1881

On November 21, Alfred Gough was hanged for the rape and murder of six-year-old Eleanor Windle.

1888

On August 10, Arthur Thomas Delaney was hanged for murdering his wife with a poker.

1889

On August 21, George Horton was hanged for murdering his eight-year-old daughter to gain £7 insurance money on her life.

1896

On August 5, William Pugh was hanged for the murder of Elizabeth Boot. She was found hacked to death with a bill hook.

1898

On December 21, John Cotton was hanged for the murder of his third wife. In the condemned cell he admitted to murdering the other two as well.

1902

On July 30, John Bedford was hanged for the murder of his girlfriend Nancy Price.

1905

On December 29, John Silk was hanged for the murder of his mother, Mary Fallon.

1906

On December 27, Walter Marsh was hanged for the murder of his wife, Eliza.

1907

On July 16, William Slack was hanged for the murder of Lucy Wilson. Lucy was murdered after she broke off her affair with William. This was the last execution to take place in Derby.

The Execution and Confession of

Hannah Bocking,

Aged 16, of Litton, near Bakewell, Derbyshire, Who suffered on Monday the 22d of March. 1819, on the New Drop, in front of the County Gaol, Derby, for wilfully Poisoning Jane Grant.

Hannah Bocking. though of so young an age, appears to have had a mind greatly darkened and depraved, for it seems that she was instigated to the dreadful crime that she committed, solely from envy and hatred to the young woman, (Jane Grant) because she lived in the family of her Grandfather-in-law, as servant, where she had herself formerly lived, and been turned away. She procured arsnic at a surgeon's in the neighbourhood, by saying, that it was for her Grandfather, for the purpose of killing Rats, and she prevailed on a young man to go with her, saying, that they would not sell it alone to her— This mortal poison she put into a spice cake, and gave it the young woman, who thanked her, and unsuspectedly eat it, but was soon after seized with dreadful pains and agonies. In her illness she was attended by her relations, and being about to expire, her dying declaration was taken, that the cake she had eaten was the cause of the torments she suffered, which dying declaration was produced at the trial, and which, connected with other strong circumstances, was satisfactory to the minds of the jury and to every person in court. So senseless and hardened in sin was this wretched creature, that she shewed no signs of remorse, nor appeared at all sensible of her awful situation when the solemn sentence of death was passed on her by the Learned Judge, but it seems that she felt severely afterwards on her return in the Caravan to the Gaol she shed many bitter tears, and continued crying for hours. It was in this situation that she confessed her crime to a Lady, distinguished for her humanity; and entirely cleared her Brother and Sister.in.law from any participation in her crime. She declared that she alone was guilty.

On the Jury returning their verdict of Guilty, the learned Judge rose and passed sentence of death upon her, that her body should be given to the surgeons to be dissected and anatomized; at the same time most solemnly expatiating upon the enormity of the unnatural crime she had committed, and the horrid light she must appear before her divine Maker, recommending a sincere repentance and a full confession of her guilt.

Since her condemnation she has been attended by the Chaplain of the Gaol, and the Rev. Mr. Leech and others; and we hope their instructions have proved beneficial to her soul. Between twelve and one o'clock she was brought in front of the county Gaol, and having spent a short time in prayer, she was launched into eternity, amidst a vast concourse of spectators, a dreadful example for all such as indulge the sin of envy, hatred, or malice. From envy, hatred, and malice, may the Lord in his grace deliver us. Amen.

" Sin has a thousand treach'rous arts,
   To practise on the mind ;
With flatt'ring looks she tempts our hearts,
   But leaves a sting behind.

With names of virtue she deceives
   The aged and the young ;
And while the heedless wretch believes,
   She makes his fetters strong.

She pleads for all the joys she brings,
   And gives a fair pretence ;
But cheats the soul of heav'nly things,
   And chains it down to sense."

MARTIN, PRINTER, LEICESTER.

63

ACCOUNT OF THE LIFE, TRIAL & BEHAVIOUR OF

Jeremiah Brandreth, William Turner and Isaac Ludlam,

Who were Executed on the New Drop, in front of the County Gaol, Derby, on Friday November 7, 1817,

FOR HIGH TREASON.

JEREMIAH BRANDRETH, alias John Coke, alias the Nottingham Captain, WILLIAM TURNER, ISAAC LUDLAM, the elder, and a number of others were brought to trial at the County Hall, in Derby, on Thursday the 16th of October, 1817.

It appeared on evidence, that a number of persons, from one to five hundred, assembled in the Parish of Southwingfield, in the County of Derby, and with Guns, Pistols, Swords, Clubs, Pikes, Bludgeons, and other offensive Weapons, maliciously and traitorously did levy and make war against our Lord the King and his Laws; and after their trials, which lasted several days, were found GUILTY of HIGH TREASON, and the following sentence passed on them:—

That you and each of you be taken to the jail from which you have been brought, and thence drawn on a hurdle to the place of execution, where you shall be severally hanged by the neck till you be dead, and afterwards your heads be severed from your bodies, and your bodies be divided into four quarters, and placed at his Majesty's disposal; and may the Lord God of all mercy have compassion upon you.

JEREMIAH BRANDRETH, aged 27, Frameworkknitter, was born at Exeter, he has left a wife and two children, who now resides at Sutton-in-Ashfield, in the County of Nottingham. A short time before his execution Brandreth's wife visited him in prison, and asked him some particulars as to his shooting Mrs. Hepworth's man, but he declined giving her any information on the subject: and being asked the reason why he had not shaved during his imprisonment, he replied, " It was not to disguise himself, but that it appeared to him more natural in that state." He was not much affected at seeing her, and she was less distressed than might have been expected.

When Brandreth was asked by the Clerk of Arraigns, what he had to say, why sentence to die should not be passed upon him, according to law, he replied,

" I would ask for mercy, if it were possible, that mercy could be extended towards me, and would address you in the words of our Saviour—If it be possible, let this cup pass from me, yet not my will, but the will of the Lord be done."

WILLIAM TURNER, aged 46, Stone Mason, was a tall man, and had been a soldier, was born at Southwingfield, in this County, and a single man. Several persons gave Turner a good character, who said they had known him for many years, and always considered him a loyal and humane man till this happened.

On Wednesday Turner took a final leave of his brothers and relations. He was at once visited by eleven persons, who left him calm, but were themselves in the greatest possible affliction.

ISAAC LUDLAM, aged 52, Stone Mason, was born at Southwingfield, in this County, has left a wife and seven children to lament his untimely end. A short time before his execution he wrote an affectionate letter to his wife, in which he recommends her to live in the fear of God, and to bring up his children in the ways of religion, which will always prove ways of pleasantness, and the end will be everlasting life.—It having been asserted in some of the public papers that he was a Dissenting Teacher, and in others that he was a Methodist Preacher: we have good authority for stating, that he never was a Methodist Preacher, nor did he ever hold any office in that body.

On Tuesday Isaac Ludlam received a visit from his wife and daughter. Mrs. Ludlam is a very respectable looking woman. Her distress on account of the situation of her husband was great in the extreme. His doom seemed death to her. Words cannot adequately describe the mournfully affecting interview. The parting moments when the husband and father gazed on the wife and child for the last time was terrible. Burning tears mingled with fond embraces, were often repeated, and the mother and the daughter left the prison in all the horrors of despair.

Since condemnation they have been regularly attended by the Rev. J. Pickering, Chaplain of the Gaol, and have for the last few days conducted themselves in a manner becoming their awful situation.—This was the first execution for " a levying of war against the King," that ever took place in Derby. We trust in God that it will also be the last.

On the morning of execution the prisoners partook of the Lord's Supper, and joined the Chaplain in fervent prayer, and we hope that their prayers were heard.

About twelve o'Clock the unhappy sufferers were brought out in front of the County Gaol, and after a short time spent in prayer, were launched into eternity, in the presence of a vast concourse of spectators, and after hanging the usual time, their bodies were taken down and their heads cut off and held up for public view, while the executioner exclaimed, " Behold the Head of a Traitor."

The untimely end of these unhappy men is an awful warning of the sad effects of walking in the way of transgressors, and of the bitter consequences of neglecting serious religion. Ludlam once in his life for a short time was connected with a religious body, but fell from his profession. Brandreth nine years ago had some religious impressions, though he unhappily suffered them to die away; but he never connected himself with any body of professing christians. Had they in sincerity followed Religion, they would have found among either the serious dissenters or the methodists, those who would have been their helpers in the way to heaven, and they might now have been loyal subjects and useful and respected christians.

WILKINS, PRINTER, DERBY, of whom the Trials may be had,—Price 2s.

ACCOUNT OF THE LIFE, TRIAL & BEHAVIOUR OF

John Brown, Thomas Jackson, George Booth, & John King,

Who were Executed on the New Drop, in front of the County Gaol, Derby, on Friday August 15, 1817,

For Setting Fire to Hay and Corn Stacks.

NOTWITHSTANDING the public execution of such a number of Criminals who have suffered within these few years, both in this and the neighbouring Counties, (hardly an Assize having passed over without some dreadful expiation being made to the offended Laws of th Country) yet we are sorry to find that they have not had the long wished for effect, by deterring men from committing those crimes, for which their lives are forfeited.—We sincerely wish this mournful scene may be attended with more happy consequences.

J. BROWN, aged 38; T. JACKSON, aged 20; G. BOOTH, aged 21; and J. KING, aged 24; were arraigned at the bar, charged on the oath of Colonel Winfield Halton, with having on the night of the 9th, or early on the morning of the 10th of Feb. last, wilfully and feloniously set fire to, and burned certain Hay and Corn Stacks, standing at Southwingfield, the property of the said Colonel W. Halton; when, after a long and impartial trial, which lasted eleven hours, the prisoners were found GUILTY, and received sentence of death.

It appeared upon evidence on the trial, that the above unfortunate men had agreed to destroy the above property, and that they met at the Four Lane Ends, near Southwingfield, on Sunday night the 9th of February, to put their design into execution; they proceeded from thence to a coal pit, not far distant, and cut a piece of thick pitch rope from one of the windlasses, which they lighted at the Whimsey; they then took the nearest way to Southwingfield, carrying the lighted rope under a hat, the night being very dark and stormy, and crossing a small river in the way, at length arrived at the stack yard with the lighted rope; and each of them being provided with a piece of candle, actually set fire to two stacks of hay and one of corn, at the same instant.

BROWN is a native of Nottingham, but has for some years past resided in and about Southwingfield, in this county, where he has left a wife and three small children to lament his untimely end.

JACKSON resided at Woolley Moor, in this county, at the time he committed the above offence, for which he has forfeited his life, and has left a wife, to whom he had been married but a short time.

BOOTH is a native of Chesterfield, but has lately resided at Wessington, near Crich, in this county, whose wife died about a year ago, by whom he had one child which is now living, and is about two years old.

KING resided at a small house near Matlock, but enlisted into the army, from which he was a deserter at the time he was apprehended for the crime for which he suffered.

Since the condemnation of these unfortunate men, they have behaved in a manner becoming their unhappy situations, and we hope that their untimely end will be a warning to young people of all descriptions, to keep holy the Sabbath-day, and refrain from bad company, which is the forerunner of destruction.

About twelve o'clock this morning the unhappy sufferers were brought out in front of the County Gaol, and after a short time spent in prayer, were launched into eternity.

HYMN.

O for an over-coming faith,
To cheer our dying hours;
To triumph o'er the monster death,
And all his frightful pow'rs.

Joyful with all the strength we have,
Our quiv'ring lips should sing;
Where is thy boasted vict'ry death,
And where the monster's sting.

If sin be pardon'd we're secure,
Death hath no sting beside;
The law gives sin its damning pow'r,
But Christ, our ransom, dy'd.

[G. Wilkins, Printer, Derby.]

THE LIFE AND EXECUTION OF
THOMAS HOPKINSON, jun.

Who suffered this Day on the New Drop, in front of the County Gaol, Derby,

For Highway Robbery.

THIS unfortunate young man, only 20 years of age, was found guilty at the late Assizes in Derby, together with John Fletcher, of stopping William Bucknall upon the Turnpike Road near Dronfield, putting him in bodily fear, and taking from his person, a purse containing twelve shillings and six-pence.

The Criminal was born at Ashover, in this County, where he resided with his Father till he was fourteen years old. The family then removed to Woolley Moor, and here it was that he formed an intercourse with abandoned companions, and commenced that profligate career which brought him to his untimely end. In the number of his wicked associates were Thomas Jackson, jun. John King, John Brown, and George Booth, who were all executed two years ago for setting fire to stacks of hay and corn in the farm-yard of Colonel Halton. Thomas Hopkinson was an accomplice in this horrid crime, and was admitted King's evidence on the trial of his companions. Their dreadful fate afforded no salutary warning to Hopkinson, who proceeded in his guilty career till he committed the crime for which the judgment of the law has thus been awfully executed upon him.

His life, though a comparatively short one, has been marked by the commission of an incredible number of offences. Of these he made a confession during his confinement in the house of correction at Chesterfield, and they are more than sufficient to shew that his whole time was spent in the perpetration of almost every species of vice. The petty pilferings in which he first engaged, gradually led him on to bolder offences; his mind became so familiarized with guilt, that he seemed scarcely sensible of its depravity; and thus in the natural progress of iniquity, he was led on till he " was driven away in his wickedness."

On looking back to the history of his short but criminal course, his first transgressions may with great justice be referred to the wicked company of Thomas Jackson, who was his constant associate. After this intimacy had been formed, every moral feeling and every religious consideration were abandoned. He no longer read his bible, he no longer went to church; and thus the seeds of instruction which had been sown in his infant mind were choked and became unfruitful. Poaching, robbing hen roosts, gardens, and barns were the occupations of his nights; and his days were spent either in that kind of idleness which is ever the fruitful source of fresh crimes, or in dissipating in profligate excess the money acquired by his nefarious practices. Offences of a still heavier kind succeeded of course to those we have enumerated. Sheep stealing, horse stealing, house breaking, and highway robbery, marked the boldness with which he and his companions advanced in vice. They were indeed the terror and the reproach of their neighbourhood. After his condemnation, Hopkinson showed not much concern for his approaching fate. The sight of the unfortunate woman in the chapel, who was going to be executed on the 22nd of March, excited in him a stronger emotion than he expressed on any other account, but he was not capable of deep reflection, and seldom seemed sufficiently impressed with the awful situation in which he himself was placed.

It is no uncommon thing for persons, who come to an untimely and disgraceful end, to acknowledge upon the fatal scaffold, that a neglect of the Sabbath, laid the foundation of their ruin.

Between twelve and one o'clock this day, he was brought to the fatal spot, and having spent a short time in prayer, he was launched into eternity, amidst a vast concourse of spectators.

(G. WILKINS, PRINTER, QUEEN STREET, DERBY.)   April 2d, 1819.

Bibliography.

Books:

Armitage J.: *Derby A History* (Amberley Publishing 2014)

Foxe J.: Actes and Monuments of these Latter and Perillous Days, Touching Matters of the Church), popularly known as Foxe's Book of Martyrs (John Day 1563)

Garner E.: *Hanged For Three Pennies* (The Breedon Books Publishing Company Ltd 2000)

Hutton W.: *History and Antiquities of the Borough of Derby Town Down to 1791* (Derby 1791)

Other sources:

British Executions - http://www.britishexecutions.co.uk/

Contemporary Execution Broadsides

Derby Mercury Newspaper – Various Editions.

Wikimedia Commons - https://commons.wikimedia.org/

Image Credits:

Book publishing image: Photo by Susan Q Yin on Unsplash

www.derbyuncovered.com

@derbyuncovered

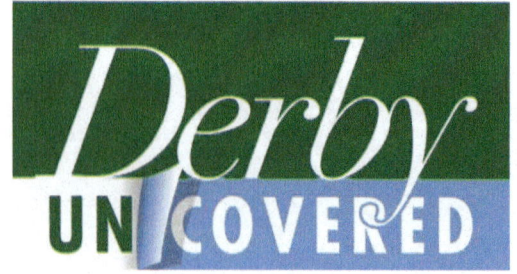

If you enjoyed this, then why not subscribe to our bi-monthly Derby Uncovered Newspaper?

Full of the very best of Derby and Derbyshire's history and heritage, it's completely free to subscribe – you only pay the postage and packaging.

Go to www.derbyshire-bazaar.com to subscribe now.

Would you like your story to be published?

All of us at Derby Uncovered believe firmly that the history of our area is created by and belongs to you - the people of the area.

We want to help you tell your stories and your history and to help us do that we have now launched our book publishing service.

Our aim is to print and publish the stories, lives and histories that you – the people of Derby and Derbyshire - have to tell.

You don't have to be a professional author - you just need to have an interesting story to tell. If you'd like to find out more about this, then please get in touch.

Coming soon!!

A Palatial Building - A short history of the Derby Hippodrome by John M. Taylor.

Derby Uncovered are excited to announce that we will soon be releasing A Palatial Building - A short history of the Derby Hippodrome by John M. Taylor.

This book offers you – the reader – the chance to take a look back at the history of the Derby Hippodrome from the its planning stages through to it closure and after.

Written by John M. Taylor – Derby's foremost Derby Hippodrome Expert – the book takes you on a wonderful journey back into Derby's past and is both wonderfully informative and incredibly hard to put down.

Keep an eye out on our social media for more details on its release.

@derbyuncovered

Printed in Great Britain
by Amazon

26173575R00044